PLAN B:

Protecting Your Career From The Winds of Change

Elwood N. Chapman

CRISP PUBLICATIONS, INC.
Los Altos, California

PLAN B:

Protecting Your Career From The Winds of Change

Elwood N. Chapman

CREDITS
Editor: **Michael G. Crisp**
Designer: **Carol Harris**
Typesetting: **Interface Studio**
Cover Design: **Carol Harris**
Artwork: **Ralph Mapson**

Copyright © 1988 by Crisp Publications, Inc.
Printed in the United States of America

Crisp books are distributed in Canada by Reid Publishing, Ltd., P.O. Box 7267, Oakville, Ontario, Canada L6J 6L6.

In Australia by Career Builders, P.O. Box 1051 Springwood, Brisbane, Queensland, Australia 4127.

And in New Zealand by Career Builders, P.O. Box 571, Manurewa, New Zealand.

Library of Congress Catalog Card Number 87-73560
Chapman, Elwood N.
Plan B: Protecting Your Career From The Winds of Change
ISBN 0-931961-48-3

> *"Life is a series of collisions with the future; it is not a sum of what we have been but what we yearn to be."*
>
> *Jose' Ortega y Gasset*

ABOUT THIS BOOK

Plan B: is not like most books. It stands out from others in an important way. It is not a book to read—it's a book to *use*. The unique ''self-paced'' format and the many exercises encourage the reader to get involved and try some new ideas immediately.

This publication will introduce innovative building-block ideas that will help you take advantage of your present job to dramatically enhance your future. Using the simple but sound system (seven steps) can head your career and life in a better direction. All you need do is give it a chance.

Plan B (and other books listed on page 91) can be used effectively in a number of ways. Here are some possibilities.

—**Individual study.** Because the book is self-instructional, all that is needed is a quiet place, some time and a pencil. By completing the activities and exercises, most readers will quickly turn their present job into a stepping stone to a more progressive and exciting career path.

—**Workshops and Seminars.** The book is effective in helping participants unlock themselves from traditional but ineffective ways to view a job or career. By formulating a Plan B, one's Plan A starts to look better while other doors of opportunity open.

—**Resource for courses concerned with career progress.** Many teachers like to add a unit to their course content that will prepare students for the winds of change that exist in the world of work. The low cost of PLAN B makes it possible for students to own their own copy.

The PLAN B is part of a series called BE TRUE TO YOUR FUTURE. Other books include a Fifty-Minute CAREER DISCOVERY program and a book titled I GOT THE JOB! See page 90 for more details.

CONTENTS

VIEW YOUR CAREER FROM A NEW PERSPECTIVE

Erase from memory any preconceived ideas you have regarding career growth and job changes and open your mind to a new, innovative approach that will help you view your career from a more exciting perspective. A career growth program (Plan B) as conceived and introduced in this book, is far more than a contingency job plan. Rather, it is a thoughtful broad-based, personal growth program that can take you to either a more significant role in your present organization, or lead you to a better position elsewhere. It will also help you focus on a motivating life goal. Best of all, this can take place while you remain in your present job. The risk is minimal.

PART I

LIFE GOALS
COME FIRST

TIE YOUR HOPES TO A BIGGER STAR

The primary reason people lose motivation to succeed in their chosen careers is often because they do not link their efforts to a life goal. Without the advantage of a ''bigger picture'' they become mired in an attitude best expressed by the old saying, ''another day another dollar''. They become stalled and feel ''boxed in''. Instead of viewing work as a vehicle that will lead them to fulfillment, they often see it as something to endure. Soon they are blaming their organization or their superiors for their lack of motivation.

Of course, when it comes to determining a life goal, it is easier said than done. Still, it need not be a frustrating, painful, or lengthey process. In fact, with a little concentration, you can start the process now.

A good way to begin is to stop looking at your current job or position as simply a regular paycheck (with certain benefits) and view it instead as a vehicle that can take you in the direction you want to go in life. At first, this may seem overwhelming, but all it really means is that you need to change the focus of your present thinking. In short, you can open and expand your mind and think bigger! Once you have a life goal, insights into what you can do to enhance your present career will improve and your motivation to succeed will be stronger and easier to maintain.

AIM HIGH

When Brad graduated from college he was excited about the future. When he landed a job as a Marketing Trainee with a national firm, he became even more enthusiastic. Three years later things turned sour. Mark felt bogged down and disenchanted. Soon he lost his self-motivation and became ineffective.

Why did it happen? Without knowing it, Mark lost sight of his future. Then, with the help of a close friend, he took time to evaluate his dreams and focus on a life goal. Result? Mark developed a more professional perspective and regained his self-motivation. Not only did he get his confidence back, but everything he did was more directed and the improved quality of his work was noticed by all.

Please do not get the idea that you must develop a highly altruistic, euphoric life goal to get results similar to that of Mark. Very few individuals can make a significant scientific discovery, win a Nobel prize, or be voted the most valuable player of a professional sports team. Your life goal will probably be a very practical thing like:

➤ raising a happy family,

 ➤ building a dream home from scratch,

  ➤ making other people happier with themselves,

   ➤ achieving recognition through creative efforts,

    ➤ creating an estate or

     ➤ preparing for a fulfilling retirement.

Everyone can develop a motivating life goal but it is vital that you accept the premise that life goals differ from other goals. For example, selecting the right career or finding the best possible job is a significant accomplishment. However, these are not life goals. Buying a home is a worthy goal, but unless there are some special circumstances (like designing and building it yourself) it is not, for most people, a life goal.

YOUR LIFE GOALS

A life goal is usually expressed as something more personal which is beyond the framework of a job or career. The ideal life goal should provide inspiration over a lifespan. It should be a daily "booster pump" to one's attitude. A life goal can make challenges (like winning a promotion or finding a better job) easier to achieve. For those with a firm grip on a meaningful life goal, there is more spirit, substance, and direction to daily living. And when times turn bad, they survive better.

BRINGING YOUR LIFE INTO FOCUS

Most people will not have as much trouble coming up with a life goal as they might expect. This is because, perhaps without knowing it, they already have one lying dormant within them. It is already *there* waiting to be brought to the surface. To help you discover a life goal, try asking yourself this question.

> WHAT DO I WANT TO ACCOMPLISH WITH THE TALENTS AND ABILITIES I POSSESS THAT WILL GIVE ME A SENSE OF LASTING FULFILLMENT?

Another approach is to project yourself into the future and imagine you are looking back on your life. Then ask yourself:

> WHAT WOULD HAVE GIVEN MY LIFE MORE MEANING?

GOALS SHOULD BE MOTIVATING

Although it may be ideal to think that a life goal must be worthy and contribute to humanity, this is not always true. Some goals, such as accumulating personal wealth, or achieving power are not altruistic. Yet they can be life goals because they are highly motivating to some people over a life span.

No other person can define a life goal for you or impose one on you. Your goal must come from within and the choice is yours alone. Most of all, you must *want* to have one.

The following exericse was designed to help you isolate and clarify a life goal. It can do this by providing examples of how other people came up with their goals and how this discovery helped them enhance their careers. Please read the profiles. When you have finished, be invited to project your own life goal at the end of the exercise. As you proceed, remember that minds are like parachutes—they don't function until they are open.

LIFE GOAL PROFILES

Listed below are examples that illustrate the significant relationship between life goals and career success. Please ☑ check the one with which you most closely identify and then write your own in the space provided at the end of this section.

☐ More than anything Jake wants money. Having grown up lacking material goods, Jake sincerely wants financial security and, ultimately, an affluent lifestyle. So strong is his desire, that he intends to remain single until his goal is well on the way to reality. Although some of his friends consider Jake to be narrow-minded and selfish, his goal has kept him self-motivated over the past ten years. Result? Jake is now a vice president for a large accounting firm.

☐ Freda has two life goals woven into a single fabric. One is to travel, the other is to promote international understanding. Freda had to struggle over a long period of time to clarify her goals. As a result, she was almost 40 when she decided to go back to school. There she took travel courses and became bilingual. When she was ready to tackle the job market her life goal gave her the competitive edge to win an outstanding opportunity with the best travel agency in town. Since then, Freda has opened her own agency and has five agents working for her. She travels about 50% of the time and feels good about doing her small bit in promoting international understanding..

LIFE GOAL PROFILES

☐ Jennifer was going nowhere with her organization until she became a born again Christian. Then, with more insight and motivation, she found a job that helped others become more self-sufficient. Today, even though her annual income is modest, she is challenged and happy. The difference? Jennifer claims it is because her goal to help others is being fulfilled. Her job is the vehicle that allows her to accomplish what is most important to her.

☐ When Matt and Joan ended their marriage, Joan's goal was to be a good parent and provider for her son Jimmy. With help from a college guidance center, she decided to prepare for and find a career in computer applications. Once started, it has been one career advance after another. What gave Joan the competitive advantage? Wanting to provide a good home for Jimmy made the difference.

☐ Raymond completed two years of college, did a hitch in the Marine Corps and worked part-time as a laborer for three years. He never gave much thought to something better. Then he met Sue. By the time they were engaged, he was working full time and on his way to becoming a journeyman carpenter. Raymond puts it this way: ''Once I wanted a future with Sue everything turned around for me. Someday I will be a contractor.''

LIFE GOAL PROFILES

☐ After 25 years as a long-haul truck driver, Jack was forced to resign because of a back injury. For two years he plugged along in a job with the same firm, washing trucks. Then he and his wife were invited to take a trip in an R.V. with friends. Result? They decided they wanted to travel in an R.V. of their own upon retirement. Today Jack is a well-paid and respected dispatcher for a major manufacturing concern. He comments: "I needed a goal to motivate me to prepare for our retirement. Now I am enjoying myself so much working we may postpone retirement a year or two."

DOING YOUR OWN PROFILE

The profiles of others you just read may help suggest the kind of profile you will eventually write for yourself. Now would be a good time to try writing a preliminary script for yourself, using the spaces below.

_____

_____

_____

_____

_____

_____

_____

_____

LIFE GOALS CAN CHANGE

Life goals are not frozen in cement. Like other things, they can change as a person matures. Even so, a tentative goal is far better than none at all. Before you consider the non-traditional career enhancement ideas to follow, it is important for you to establish a tenatative life goal. If you fail to do this, you may need the book, agree with the ideas, but never do anything to put them into operation.

On the next page is a diagram you are encouraged to complete. The star in the middle is designed to contain three life goals. If you wish you can settle for one or two.

Once you have recorded your goal or goals, you are ready to take advantage of the Plan B Growth Program described in the pages ahead.

TIE YOUR CAREER GROWTH PROGRAM TO LIFE GOALS

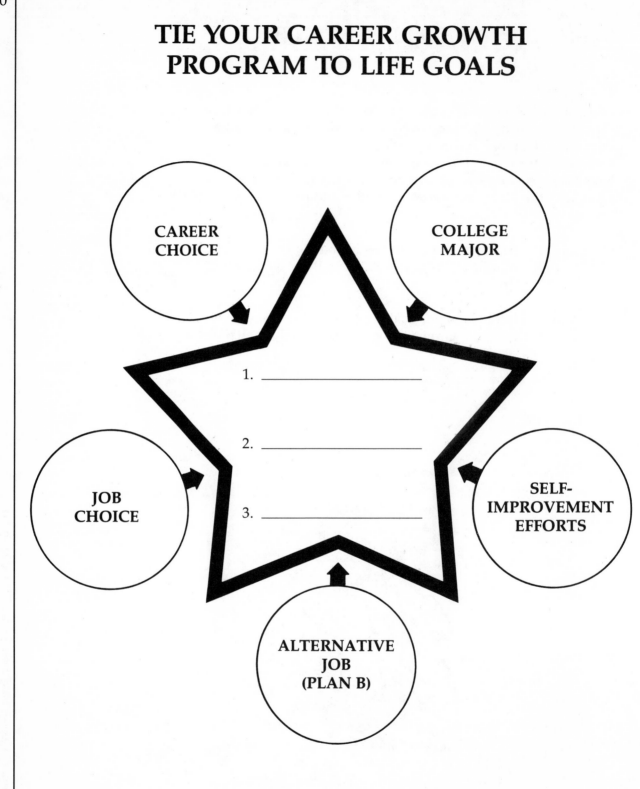

CAREER CHOICE

COLLEGE MAJOR

1. _____

2. _____

3. _____

JOB CHOICE

SELF-IMPROVEMENT EFFORTS

ALTERNATIVE JOB (PLAN B)

PART II

PLAN B AND THE WINDS OF CHANGE

LORI

When Lori first heard a friend of hers describe the psychological advantages of having a written Plan B, she was skeptical. To Lori a Plan B was nothing more than a general plan to keep in the back of your mind in case you lost your job. Lori's friend persisted and Lori eventually won out. This is the way Lori now describes a Plan B:

"One of the 'laws of life' seems to be that the moment you don't have medical insurance, you break your leg; when you don't have auto insurance, you have an accident. I view having a Plan B in the same way. When you have the job security that only an alternate growth program can provide, chances are good you won't need it. But having the protection provides a sense of confidence. It is nice to feel you don't really need another job but know you are ready if things change. It comes down to what insurance people call 'risk management'. By protecting your future, it creates a whole different attitude toward your present work."

WHAT IS A PLAN B?

Plan B is nothing more than a career insurance policy. Properly developed, it will provide a cushion against the shocks of future changes, such as unexpected unemployment. A plan B as described in this book, is a carefully researched and designed strategy to provide an immediate and exciting opportunity should your present job (Plan A) lose its luster or disappear. A Plan B is not a temporary alternative or substitute job should problems arise. It is a reserve program that can match or be superior to your Plan A (present job). And it is more!

View Plan B as having a large sum of money salted away in an investment of your choice. You may never draw on the account, but it is there if you become unhappy with your present situation. And, just as well invested money draws interest or pays dividends while held in reserve, so does a Plan B. For example, the very existance of a Plan B growth program can cause you to feel more independent (and secure) about your present job. This in turn, can cause you to be more confident and thereby do better at it. It can also give your present job (whatever it may be) more meaning and help you make progress toward a life goal. These, and other significant benefits to be explored in the pages ahead, are not normally seen or understood. But they exist and can guarantee that you receive a high rate of interest from your investment. In other words, a Plan B growth program will add new assets to your ''career bank.''

Despite these and other advantages, most people wait on the sidelines without developing a diversified career ''contingency plan.'' In doing this, they put all of their career eggs into one basket. This is foolish when you consider that a Plan B can help a Plan A prosper.

THE ANATOMY OF A PLAN B

A Plan B is a comprehensive, detailed, and realistic career plan that can be activated within a few days. It is a seven step strategy that has been planned in advance so if your present job (Plan A) disappears, or you wish to leave it behind, you have replacement choices. These will be in harmony with your abilities, talents, interests, and life goals.

A Plan B growth program is more than an idea in the back of your mind. It must be fully researched and planned in writing. Key contacts must also be developed as your Plan B is formulated. Although it may sound like doing a homework assignment, it is far more exciting and the benefits are greater and more immediate. Ideally, your Plan B can be developed while you are improving your Plan A. Many successful people devote several hours each week over a period of months to develop and refine a high quality Plan B.

And they enjoy the challenge!

THE WINDS OF CHANGE

For many people a Plan B would have been a good idea twenty years ago. But, then few people were thinking in that direction. Ten years ago such a plan would have been an excellent strategy. Those who developed one outdistanced others. Today Plan B is virtually mandatory. Read the daily paper and you soon realize there is no immunity from changes that can render either your job or your organization obsolete.

What our parents used to call a ''secure job'' is extinct. Changes have been so dramatic in recent years that even if you own and operate a small business, economic, social, political or legal changes can suddenly throw you into bankruptcy. Perhaps trends change, or maybe rent or insurance rates explode. Life simply doesn't come with guarantees.

Alvin Toffler in his book *Future Shock* (published in 1971) predicted changes that seemed revolutionary. Many of the changes he predicted arrived so fast that Mr. Toffler published a second book soon thereafter titled *The Third Wave* to catch up on the wild winds of change. Toffler did an outstanding job describing the large changes to the country. Most people were unable, however, to consider how those changes would affect their lives. Only a few individuals took Toffler's predictions personally.

In addition to external changes (such as those described by Toffler) there are changes within individuals. Sometimes a person reaches a ''crisis point'' where a new life goal appears and career adjustments need to be made. At other times, job dissatisfaction becomes accute and a change becomes a necessity.

Are the winds of change blowing in your life today? What impact will they have on your future? On the following pages are some causes (winds) that may sweep you off your feet.

Are you ready for them?

WINDS THAT COULD BLOW YOUR JOB AWAY

RESTRUCTURING: Almost all major organizations are streamlining to lower overhead and become more competitive. World competition for established markets are responsible. Some organizations started this process earlier than others. They were wise. The result for these organizations was more gradual change and fewer layoffs. Today, no organization is immune. Everyone has had to adjust. Some firms have helped retrain employees for new jobs; others have simply cut their workforce. This "downsizing" has had a sobering effect upon employee morale. Some of the more fortunate employees received special severance incentives (known as "golden handshakes") or were provided with professional "outplacement counseling" to help them adjust. Others were simply handed a "pink slip" and left to fend for themselves. Very few of those laid-off had a workable Plan B in the wings.

MERGERS: in a merger two organizations decide to join forces to become more efficient or enter new markets. Often one company is in financial trouble and is taken over by a healthy corporation. The term often used during a merger is consolidation. Savings occur when two offices are combined into one. But people pay the price because two sets of employees, (such as office staff) are not usually needed. Someone has to go or change jobs and seniority or talent do not always count.

CHANGES-CHANGES-CHANGES

DISLOCATIONS: Economic pressures sometimes make it necessary for an organization to relocate its offices or plants. Sometimes organizations move from New York because of high salaries and rent to less expensive places such as Texas, or Kentucky. It makes good sense economically, but in the process many people are left behind. Often many can't (or won't) move. They resist the winds of change. If they do not have a Plan B in reserve, they must scramble.

POLITICAL: Everyone is familiar with political change. Smart people always have a Plan B in Washington, D.C., Partisan employees face the strongest political winds. Civil Service provides job security, but even here changes are being considered. Political winds accelerate economic and social changes that can affect everyone.

SOCIAL: Double income families are more vulnerable to change than when there is a single wage earner. If the primary breadwinner loses his or her job, it often means this person has to find suitable employment elsewhere. Result? Two people need a Plan B rather than one. Social winds have indirectly created a greater need for alternative career plans.

COMPETITION FROM IMMIGRANTS: The American economy is not only adjusting to foreign competition on products, it also faces competition from immigrants. We have a growing number of people from other nations joining our workforce. Many are willing to work harder than the typical American worker and consequently they absorb entry level jobs which can be a springboard to more responsible positions later.

All of the winds of change mentioned add up to a compelling need for smart workers to have a well-designed Plan B. It is no longer *if* you get caught up on the whirlwind of change that might result in a change in your job status, it is being prepared for *when*.

JULIE

Julie was so tired of rumors about cutbacks that there was a certain amount of relief when her firm finally declared bankruptcy and eliminated her position. She immediately signed up for unemployment insurance payments and took a two-week "vacation". Then she started a job hunting expedition.

Things didn't go well. For one thing, Julie wasn't prepared mentally for a job search. Even worse, she had allowed some of her basic skills to deteriorate. As a result, Julie became discouraged and lost her confidence. It took her over a year (including several college classes) to get her once promising career back on track.

Julie made the classic mistake of thinking she could use unemployment insurance as a security blanket. She felt a new job would be easy to find. What she failed to understand is that developing a Plan A from scratch is far more difficult than developing a Plan B while you are still working. If Julie had worked on a fleasible growth program before her position was eliminated, she could have enjoyed her vacation and returned prepared to locate a better position than she left. With a solid Plan B her one year "down period" would have been eliminated.

If you dislike trying to find a job on a full-time basis, a growth program prepared ahead of time is your best possible strategy.

PLAN B BEGINS
WITH A PHILOSOPHY

It would be a mistake to consider a career growth program (prepared while in your present job) simply as a blueprint to take you through a difficult transition period into another job or career. It is equally important to view such a plan as an attitude. The mind set for Plan B says one must not depend exclusively on others (especially managers in large organizations) to develop and protect your future. A good Plan B is a "take care of yourself" project. It is an attitude that acknowledges change is inevitable and no job or career is 100% secure. It is an attitude that recognizes the danger in becoming too comfortable with any career role and the acceptance that alternatives are necessary to avoid becoming vulnerable to the winds of change.

Obviously, change can be a barrier from reaching a life goal. Change can send a person on a detour from which a return to the main highway is difficult. Thus a Plan B philosophy says: "No matter how strong the winds may be, you cannot allow them to blow away your future. You must ride out the storm, adjust, and be true to your future."

Plan B is basically a way to interpret the modern world which will give you a better chance to reach your life goals. The "good old days" of company loyalty, and promotion from within, are not as realistic as they once were. The rules have changed. The game is played differently. And without a Plan B you risk leaving yourself open to frustration and despair.

The good news about constructing a career growth program is that the philosophy you develop will enhance other aspects of your life. Some examples of this are provided on the next page.

THE PLAN B HABIT

Some years ago my wife and I were traveling in Europe when student riots in France prevented us from following our scheduled plan. Stranded in London, and feeling sorry for ourselves, we came up with an alternate plan to visit Scotland. We had a glorious time and that experience caused us to form the "Plan B" habit.

Although the material in this book deals with the benefits of developing a career Plan B (and how to do it), you will also see the advantages in other situations. For example, a Plan B is desirable:

- When a financial reverse occurs.
- When another individual lets you down.
- When unexpected company arrives.
- When a college major turns sour.
- When your dentist retires.
- When your favorite restaurant is closed.
- When a computer fails.
- When your car breaks down.
- When your flight is cancelled.

Almost every plan you make could use a Plan B to provide flexibility and prevent frustration. In developing a Plan B for career and life goal purposes, you will see the advantages (and improve your skills) in having a backup strategy in every day situations. Result? The unexpected "bumps" of living will be easier to handle.

THOSE WITH A PLAN B IN PLACE USUALLY WIND UP HAPPIER IN THE WORKPLACE AND LESS SUSCEPTIBLE TO JOB BURNOUT

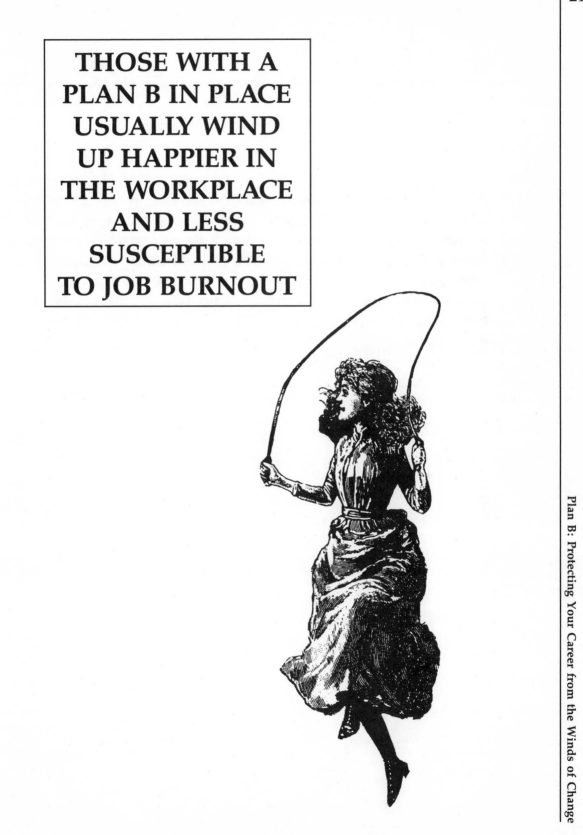

THE CHALLENGE!

The foundation of the Plan B philosophy is the development of a learning attitude that says: "I will start learning more about my specific career area and the opportunities it provides from a variety of sources. These sources include key people I know or will meet in the future. It means learning more about my present job including seminars and self-learning. I accept that only by keeping my skills current can I avoid a major "catch up" period in the future–a period that could measurably slow my career progress.

THE SEVEN STEP STRATEGY

ANTICIPATING THE WINDS OF CHANGE

This section contains seven steps that will lead you through a successful Plan B growth program. Although all seven steps are recommended, you may decide to eliminate one or two or place more emphasis on some. Every situation is different. Each individual has his or her own form of interpretation and style. After all, the future you are dealing with is your own!

YOU'LL NEVER COMPLETE
A PLAN B IF YOU
VIEW IT AS WORK–
YOU'VE GOT ENOUGH
OF THAT ALREADY.
TIE IT TO YOUR LIFE
GOAL AND MAKE
IT A CHALLENGE.
IT CAN EVEN BE FUN!

THE SEVEN STEP STRATEGY

STEP 1
COUNT DOWN!

(How to design a support system to help you complete a Plan B.)

Few individuals who promise themselves to complete a growth plan actually do so because they lack a support system. Without such a system it is easy for a Plan B to become "just talk".

> Genevieve had slowly turned off her friends and co-workers through constant talk about getting a teaching credential, but never doing anything about it. Her best friend, Rachel, finally decided to address the situation and said: "Look, Gen, we are all tired of talk without any action. Why don't you do something about your future or forget it? I'll make you a wager. When you get your credential I'll buy you dinner at the best restaurant in town. Between now and then, promise you won't keep talking about how you're going to get your credential. Deal?"

Like Genevieve, most people need all the motivation they can muster to start and complete a Plan B. What kind of motivation would you require? And equally important, what kind of support from others would be necessary to convert what is in your mind to action? On the next page are four options. If you feel that one is the kind of support you would favorably respond to, place a check in the appropriate square. If none appeal to you, design your own plan in the spaces provided.*

---

*Should the reader feel that a support system of any kind is unnecesary, he or she is reminded that a Plan B must be developed while a Plan A is kept in full operation and one's lifestyle is maintained. It is something you do on top of everything else. It is not business as usual and that is why an advance support strategy (especially if there is some excitement to it) may be best for some people.

DESIGN A SUPPORT SYSTEM

☐ **Option #1: USE THE POWER OF SECRECY.** For some individuals, getting others to provide support would demonstrate weakness on their part and do more harm that good. These people like to prove to others, (especially superiors), that they are independently strong and disciplined. Thus the more secrecy surrounding the project the more motivated these individuals become. It is the fact that they do not discuss their Plan B with others until they can make a big announcement at the end (after completion) that provides the motivating goal.

☐ **Option #2: COMMIT YOURSELF TO OTHERS.** This option is in juxtoposition to number one. Some individuals find the movitation they require is obtained by openly communicating their plan to those most important in their lives. Not having to ''back down'' from a commitment (and winding up with the ''guilts'') is what causes these people to complete a project. They purposely create their own trap and then make certain they are not caught in it!

☐ **Option #3: ARRANGE A PERSONAL CONTRACT.** This works when there is a significant person who is willing to provide support and counseling on a regular basis. Spouses, close friends, or mentors work well. The idea is to make a verbal (or written) agreement to meet at regular intervals to evaluate progress until the Plan B is complete. For many individuals, this options works well.

☐ **Option #4: CHOOSE A SMALL, SELECT SUPPORT GROUP.** Those who prefer this approach like to share their Plan B with a select group of individuals who can be called upon for guidance and support. It is like doing a long-distance swim and having people at both ends and along your side to cheer you on as you make the effort. Structure in the form of regular progress reports can be added if desired. Here again, care in the selection of support people is critical. Only those who will take the assignment seriously should be given consideration.

☐ **Option #5: DOING IT WITH OTHERS.** For some a partnership or team arrangement is the best of all. Besides the fun that can occur sharing and working together, mutual support is nice to have. The primary problem with a ''partnership approach'' is that one party may be more serious and professional than the other to produce a viable Plan B. A team or partnership effort may work, but it may be wise to reserve one of the other options in case is doesn't.

☐ **Option #6: SELF-DESIGNED STRATEGY.** Please write out the option you prefer. If desired, use a combination of those suggested above.

_____

_____

_____

_____

_____

Once you have your support system in place you are ready to prepare a Plan B for launching at a later date. The more you anticipate this event the more motivated you will be to get there!

CASE 1: RICHARD

When Richard came home from Viet Nam it was his Uncle George who introduced him to the President of Barr Manufacturing who offered Richard a job. Since then Richard has made slow but steady progress with Barr. He is now Traffic Manager (and loves it) but is worried for two reasons. (1) He needs to measurably upgrade his statistical skills to keep the job. (2) Rumor has it that Barr may sell out to a larger company.

Richard has been thinking about developing a Plan B for two years but lacks enough motivation to get started. Last night, in a discussion with his wife Marie, it was decided he should adopt one of these strategies.

(1) Ask Uncle George if he will sign an informal contract that commits Richard to report on his progress every two weeks. Richard has so much respect for his Uncle that it would be most difficult to let him down. Besides, Uncle George is knowledgable and could provide expert guidance until his Plan B is finished.

(2) Create a small support group by asking the following individuals if they would be available to talk with him should his progress "bog down".

> –Marie
> –His superior at work with whom he has a "mentor" type relationship.
> –Jack, his best friend.
> –Neighbor Fred who is a retired teacher.
> –Uncle George

Which strategy would you support?

_____

_____

_____

See page 83 for author's comments.

STEP 2
HEDGE YOUR CAREER BET

(Free yourself to do a Plan B by streamlining your Plan A)

Frequently an individual will fix up a home or autombile to sell, then, after the improvements have been made, change his or her mind. The home or car turns out to be better than what is available for the same price in the marketplace. Why not keep it?

The same thing can happen in preparing a growth plan. When you have finished with it, your Plan A (present job) looks so much better than when you started you decide to keep it. This is most apt to occur when you streamline your Plan A to work on Plan B.

> When Jill first heard a friend say the best way to get ready to leave a job is to become better at it, she almost flipped. Yet, after discussing the idea at length Jill agreed. The premise is basic. By becoming more effective at Plan A it ceases to be a drag on the preparation of a Plan B. Then, if Plan B does not work out, you can fall back on an improved Plan A and still come out ahead. Some people call this hedging. Jill decided to follow this strategy.

It stands to reason that developing a workable Plan B will take time, energy, and mental effort. But does it need to be a burden? The answer is no, providing you relieve some of the pressure by becoming more effective in your present job. In other words, streamline what you do so you become more efficient and it takes less out of you.

As contradictory as it may at first seem, your second step is to improve the way you are dealing with your Plan A. To assist you in doing this twenty possible efficiency measures are listed on the next page. It is recognized that work situations are vastly different, so some of the suggestions may not apply.

STREAMLINING YOUR PLAN A

Place a check in a few of the boxes listed below and you will be gaining time to work more seriously on your Plan B.

☐ Curtail excessive socialization on the job. Stay friendly but back away a little.

☐ Concentrate on your job and let others worry about problems beyond your control.

☐ Become more professional as a worker. Look and act the part.

☐ Become a more positive person. Let negative views and rumors bounce off you.

☐ Work hard to increase personal productivity. A drop in your productivity can be counter-productive in building a Plan B.

☐ Work to restore any negative relationships that exist. These cause an energy drain which could be put to better use elsewhere.

☐ Eliminate obvious time-wasters that have become habits (such as an afternoon coffee break).

☐ Insulate yourself against unsolvable human problems that are draining you.

☐ Do a better job of balancing home and career responsibilities.

☐ If you are a manager, start delegating more. If you are not a manager spend less time carrying the work load of others.

☐ Take a stronger stand with superiors on accepting new responsibilities. Refuse to let others unload on you. Carry your full share of work but take a firm stand against overloads.

SIMPLIFY

☐ Use your lunch break (or other down time) to work on Plan B.

☐ Start building stronger relationships with those who may be in a position to help you launch your Plan B later.

☐ Start an exercise program.

☐ Improve your absentee record.

☐ Establish (in writing) daily work priorities.

☐ Whatever it takes to build a better relationship with your supervisor, do it. The less strain that falls on you from above the easier the building of your Plan B will be.

☐ Shorten business telephone conversations. Cut back on personal calls.

☐ Dress for success. Looking more efficient may help you become more efficient.

Your goal is to develop a Plan B that will improve your career, get you a better job, and take you closer to your life goal. With less stress coming from your Plan A you will be free to do this and improve your future.

If it sounds like too much work, talk it over with a support person. Perhaps there is some way you can convert the streamlining you have in mind to a challenge with a reward at the end.

CASE 2: CONFLICT

Although James and Gregg are good friends they occasionally get into some highly emotional arguments over career strategies. Yesterday, over lunch, they had a beauty when Gregg said.

"James, you might as well quit now, take a vacation, and come back looking for a new job. You miss the whole idea of using your present job as a platform to gain a better one. You can't seem to get it through your brain that becoming better at what you are doing here will improve your attitude toward outside opportunities. Right now you are cutting off your nose to spite your face."

"Look big shot", replied James, "you don't know how negative I have become about this job. I feel I am in a pressure cooker and management is turning the gas higher. Then, you sit there and tell me to take a fresh look at what I am dong to benefit myself. My guess is that 95% of people who turn sour on a job quit without having a decent plan. That's the way the system works. The only way I am going to benefit myself is to quit and take that vacation you are talking about. I will never prepare for another job until the pressure is totally off me here. As far as I am concerned, you can take your Plan B and stuff it in your ear."

Would you defend James or Gregg? Write your answer in the space below and then compare your answers to that of the author on page 83.

_____

_____

_____

STEP 3
YOU'VE GOT TO BE KIDDING!

(Your present job can provide more than money or benefits while you work on your Plan B)

This step encourages you to view your current job as a place where you can continue to learn. This holds true even if you feel boxed in, or mad at your boss, or even if you don't expect to hang around for long.

Some employees become so discouraged about their current jobs that they do not recognize some of the on-site learning opportunities that are present. A few, once they become serious about a Plan B, take a second look and discover a wide variety of learning opportunities exist. When this happens, they often reverse their previous attitude and start improving old skills while learning new ones. Of course, this doesn't happen to everyone. Rather than viewing their Plan A as a paid learning station for the duration (the smart approach) some people continue to see it as a bummer-job leading nowhere. These individuals needlessly victimize themselves.

Streamlining your Plan A (Step 2) may have already contributed to a more positive attitude toward your current job and this may have uncovered some learning opportunities you have failed to see in the past. If so, step in and learn all you can. Continue to search for new assignments and new relationships with people who have something important to teach you. The more you learn, the better things will turn out for you in the future. Easy to say, hard to do!

PSYCHOLOGICAL BLOCKS

One reason you may not have taken advantage of learning opportunities in the past is because you may have some psychological ''blocks'' to overcome. For example, blocks frequently occur among mature employees in a high tech field (like computer science). These individuals are fully capable of learning new technology but have permitted the never ending advancement of technology to form barriers in their mind and they give up.

There are three steps to overcoming learning blocks: (1) Recognize you may have one. (2) Make up your mind reverse the problem. (3) Find help to master what needs to be learned.

There is another kind of mental block. When a change occurs in the work environment some employees always seem to consider it bad no matter what the change may be. As a result, they develop a negative attitude (mental block) against it. Other colleagues have learned to view change as an opportunity not a problem. This attitude allows them to open their minds, learn new methods or skills and prepare for better jobs ahead. These individuals are not just ''putting in time'', they are preparing themselves for the future.

What can you learn from your present job? It depends upon where you are, the freedom you have, and what new learning opportunities surround you. Sometimes, after careful analysis, you may discover your job environment may not provide any new learning opportunities despite your best effort. If this turns out to be the case, you should move on to step 5.

LEARNING SOURCES

To help you identify learning sources from your present job, please complete the following exercise. Place a ✓ opposite any learning opportunity that can be developed.

☐ Ask your supervisor for some new responsibilities where new learning possibilities exist. One idea is to start with a task co-workers do not want.

☐ Go on record requesting to learn how to operate a piece of equipment or software, where you have little or no experience. Sometimes it is possible to learn this on your own time.

☐ Investigate the opportunities of company sponsored seminars or training that you can attend or take.

☐ Ask a colleague who is a specialist to help you develop some new skills.

☐ Identify accessible individuals whom you can learn from through informal meetings, interviews, and coffee breaks. Some people are better resources than books.

Each work environment has its own learning opportunities. All it takes is a motivated person who is willing to discover and absorb knowledge. This usually means asking the right questions at the right time from the right people. Although formal education and self-learning outside of work will also contribute to your future, there is nothing that can replace the on-the-job training and experience most organizations provide.

> ## It's nice to earn
> ## while you learn.

CASE 3: ATTITUDE REVERSAL

When Tanya started with her firm two years ago she made some serious mistakes. First, she learned only what was necessary for her to get the basic job done. Nothing extra. Second, she made some unnecessary human relation errors. As a result, she is currently at odds with her supervisor and has a serious conflict with two co-workers. Because she got herself off to such a bad start, Tanya has decided to develop a Plan B.

Tanya's first move was to start taking advantage of learning opportunities she neglected in the past. This included qualifying to operate three pieces of office equipment with which she was unfamiliar. She also recognized a need for greater concentration on her English skills to reduce her level of mistakes. Finally, Tanya decided to work hard to improve her relationship with her supervisor and co-workers. Tanya admits that doing all of this will mean a major behavioral change on her part, but she views it as an integral part of developing a Plan B. Besides, it is never too late to change.

What success do you predict for Tanya?

☐ Tanya will become discouraged and leave her job before her Plan B is complete.

☐ Tanya will succeed and after her Plan B is complete she will move on to a much better job.

To compare your views to that of the author, please turn to page 83.

STEP 4
QUALIFY FIRST!

(Then and only then are you officially in the race.)

In most athletic contests (cycling races, 10K's, swimming events etc.) one must qualify to compete for the recognition and prizes offered. The same is true in the career race. To qualify, a person must verify and reach current job skill standards. Those who do not do this may *think* they are in the race, but the truth is they have disqualified themselves before starting.

Every job specialty has its own compentency standards. A compentency is nothing more than a skill that can be observed and measured. There are technical skills *and* human relations skills. Although human-relations skills are not as easy to quantify as technical skills, they are equally important.

The problem with job compentencies in a dynamic society is that they are constantly upgraded by the job market. Professionals understand this and strive to keep their skills up to standard or above. Non-professionals allow their compentencies to slip.

Both Hazel and Florence use applications software in their positions as financial analysts. Hazel has a great attitude toward learning. Through self-instruction and formal classes she keeps current with the newest software. Florence, has a get-by learning attitude. She depends greatly on the help of others to keep her job.

If both of their jobs should be eliminated, Hazel would be ''market ready'' for another job. Florence would not.

WHERE ARE YOU?

Where are you? Do you need to do a market skills analysis to see if you have fallen behind in your specialty? If so, this effort should be a part of your Plan B program. To assist you in doing this, the following three part strategy is recommended.

FIRST Write out what you believe to be the present competencies required to keep you competitive in your job speciality. Include both technical and human skills.

_____

_____

_____

_____

_____

_____

_____

_____

_____

VERIFY

NEXT Verify your list by consulting with placement or human resource professionals (your local college counselor can help direct you to such a person). This, in effect, will constitute a skill analysis. Add new competencies you need to learn. Delete those no longer required.

THEN Make a list of any competencies where upgrading is required to make you competitive.

_____

_____

_____

_____

_____

_____

_____

CASE 4: JACK'S PROBLEM

When Jack finally got around to verifying the skills he would need to compete effectively for a job that was consistent with his life goal, he realized just how far behind he was. He knew some upgrading was due when he started, but when he took a close look at his list, Jack was tempted to give up.

Then it occured to him that he had two options. His first option would be to divide the competencies he needed into three groups. In Group 1 Jack would include those skills he could learn from his present job; Group 2 would include those competencies he could learn from self-study efforts at home; Group 3 would include those that he could learn only from more formal training, probably from evening courses at the local college.

His second option would be to quit his present job and return to campus full time. In this manner he could "catch up" more quickly and then start over with a new job. This option would put a strain on Jack's finances and curtail his lifestyle but would not be impossible.

What other factors should Jack consider in making his decision? Which option would you recommend? Why?

Compare your thinking with the author's on page 83.

STEP 5
DECISION TIME

(What will it be? Back to campus, self-instruction or both?)

When it comes to reaching new competency goals in order to maintain market mobility, most people have a choice. They can either go on campus (enroll in a night program) or undertake a self-instructional program at home. Once you have given careful consideration to the factors below you are invited to make the decision that is best for you.

FORMAL TRAINING AS A BRIDGE TO PLAN B

Most people find it necessary or advisable to obtain academic preparation to reach their Plan B. Sometimes (as in obtaining a license to practice medicine) this preparation can take years. Some professions require a degree to qualify for entry. At other times, a single course can do the trick.

Consider the following cases.

Jason's Plan B is to become a second level manager for a State agency. So far Jason has taken advantage of every in-service training program available. He also asks for additional responsibilities when there is some "new learning" involved. But Jason faces a serious problem in the future because he cannot speak Spanish. Co-workers and clients are increasingly Hispanic. Two weeks ago Jason enrolled in Spanish I at a local community college. He knows reaching his Plan B depends upon his becoming bilingual.

Six years ago Joan was a secretary in an architectural firm. Today she is an architect in the same organization. Developing a Plan B is responsible for the transition. Joan realized her career at that firm was at a dead-end. Six years ago, she started fooling with a Plan B and, as a result, took a course called Architecture I at a local state college. The instructor was so enthusiastic and understanding that Joan became hooked. With the full cooperation of her firm, she completed the total curriculum. Academic training was her bridge between being a secretary and an architect.

Beth (a saleswoman in a department store) and her husband Ken (a bank manager) designed a program to establish a small business of their own. Their academic preparation consisted of taking a college course at night called Successful Small Business Operation. The course project consisted of setting up a hypothetical business on paper. The professor allowed Beth and Ken to work as a team. When the course was over Beth quit her job first to get things started while Ken's salary continued. Ken joined Beth after two years. Although the academic training was minimal, without it Beth and Ken would not have received the necessary foundation to establish a successful business.

RETURN TO CAMPUS?

Does your Plan B involve additional formal education? If so, it should be encouraging for you to know the many advantages (some you may not be aware of) of returning to any campus that can provide what you need. These advantages apply whether or not you already have a degree. Please ☑ any of the benefits listed below which you were not aware of when you started the exercise.

☐ In some *career fields* college is the best place to increase compentency.

☐ Many adults who return to college do so with great anxiety, however, it is hard to find anyone later who regretted the decision.

☐ A college campus is an ideal place to network.

☐ Every person can improve his or her ability to communicate. A college campus is a great place to accomplish this goal.

☐ College professors often make excellent mentors.

☐ Colleges provide a wide variety of support services (including those taking a single course). These services include learning centers where individual tutoring is available, career guidance centers, job-placement counseling, etc. A college campus is often the best source for such services.

☐ Colleges offer many short non-credit courses so individuals can upgrade themselves at a modest cost.

☐ Graduation from high school is not always a requirement for entrance to a college program.

☐ Colleges often help their students improve self-esteem.

DO-IT-YOURSELF LEARNING

Self-study is a growing way to reach competency goals contained in a Plan B. Michelle is a case in point.

Michelle has just about exhausted the learning opportunities in her present job. Because she is a single parent raising two children, she cannot easily attend courses at the local university. She has not, however, lost her enthusiasm for her Plan B. Two or three nights each week, after the children are in bed. Michelle devotes a minimum of one hour to her own self-development. She selects publications that will lead in the direction of her Plan B. Currently she is taking a correspondence course in Beginning Supervision. Michelle's goal is to become an Administrative Officer in the small school district where she is employed.

In discussing her self-development program with her boss, Michelle made this statement: ''Reading and studying self-help books fits into my lifestyle. After the day is over and there is some quiet time, I can sit down with a cup of coffee and make excellent progress. Sometimes I can apply what I have learned the following day. My future plans do not call for an academic degree but, if needed in the future, I can list the self-help subjects covered in my resume just as if I had attended a class. Some people who find it impossible to attend formal college classes give up on future progress. This is foolish. Self-learning has many advantages. You pick your own subjects and set your own pace. Of course, it takes self-discipline but what kind of education doesn't?''

All you need do is visit your local public library or a commercial book store and browse through the various self-help books that are available for your consideration. As an example, the publisher of this book specializes in self-study books. A list of those books can be found on page 91.

IT IS POSSIBLE TO DO BOTH!

Of course, some individuals (in addition to what they learn on the job), return to campus for courses and engage in self-instructional programs at the same time. These people wisely design their own curriculum to meet their specific goals. As a guide to your own educational program please complete the following:

I plan to return to campus to complete these courses:

_____

_____

_____

I plan to use self-help publications to upgrade myself in these areas:

_____

_____

_____

Lifelong learning has become a reality. To those in retirement, learning for the sake of learning is an enviable attitude; for those who remain in the workplace new learning is often a necessity. The winds of change dictate the curriculum.

IT IS A MISTAKE TO ASSUME YOUR PRESENT COMPETENCIES WILL TAKE YOU ALL THE WAY TO RETIREMENT

CASE 5: A CHALLENGE FOR MARY

Mary accepted a position as a clerk/receptionist with a major supermarket organization because it was the only job immediately available as her husband started a new legal practice. Mary figures the Liberal Arts degree she had would stand her in good stead even though her clerical skills were underdeveloped.

Mary soon became intrigued with the Marketing Department and decided her creative talents could be put to good use in that area. As a receptionist she knew Ralph Dillon, Vice President in charge of marketing. One morning as Mr. Dillon entered the building she asked if she could speak with him. He gave her a time to meet. The meeting determined the following skills that Mary would need to achieve before she would be a candidate to join the marketing department.

> High level knowledge of applications software.
> More graphics experience in layout and design.
> A course in market research.
> Better understanding of coupon marketing.
> A course on consumer behavior.

Overwhelmed by the list, Mary decided to think twice about the idea. A few days later, Mr. Dillion saw Mary and said, "You would already have some of the skills we discussed had you been a marketing major, but frankly, I like the creativity of your liberal arts background. All of the skills we listed can be learned at night at our local university or through some self-help materials I can provide. Are you still interested?"

Does this constitute a good Plan B for Mary? What suggestions would you make as far as implementation? Please write out your answers and compare with those on page 84.

STEP 6
CREATIVE NETWORKING

To win a better job it is recommended that you seek the professional assistance of a qualified placement agency. Their contacts may help you, especially if you have an application and resume.

Although placement agencies have helped thousands of people, never forget that the best strategy is to depend upon yourself. Translated, this means you should think of yourself as your own employment agency. There are employers who are seeking people with certain skills. Just like an employment agency, you will gain your best results by marketing yourself through creative networking.

You have a major advantage over others because you have completed a Plan B. Although you may not have thought about it, your plan can constitute the secret formula you need. The following four strategies will help you establish your own ''employment agency.''

FOR THOSE NEW TO NETWORKING

Networking involves building relationships with knowledgable professionals in your career area of interest who are in a position to lead you to a new and better job opportunity. You may include placement directors on your networking list but most should be people in the field to which you aspire. Some may be in your present company. Others may work for competitors.

Relationships you build should be mutually rewarding. This means you must look for ways to repay them (if only in gratitude) so they are willing to go out of their way to assist you.

Building such a network should start as early as possible, because you may need these key individuals to help you market your plan once it is complete. How do you go about networking? Here are some suggestions. Place a ☑ opposite those you can be enthusiastic about.

☐ Joining a trade or professional association in your career area. Attend meetings. Make new friends. Learn what is going on. Where the career opportunities are.

☐ Attend conferences where you can meet other professionals in your area. Find out about any Plan B's they have.

☐ Attend formal classes, seminars, or workshops and make new friends so you can exchange career information with them.

☐ Make the effort to create a mentor or two within your present organization.

☐ Start spending time with some Plan B enthusiasts in your or other organizations.

☐ Contact professionals and arrange informational interviews to gain their suggestions on how to activate your Plan B when it is ready.

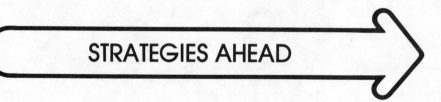

STRATEGIES AHEAD

STRATEGY 1
BECOME A CAREER
INFORMATION MAGNET

First you need to understand what is going on in the marketplace of your career specialty. What changes are taking place? What needs are not being filled? What new areas of expertise are employers seeking? What salary and benefit packages are being offered?

There are many ways to accumulate this kind of data. Check those below that have appeal.

☐ Become more active in trade associations. Attend meetings with "networking" in mind.

☐ Join other, related trade associations.

☐ Have lunch or after-work social meetings with knowledgeable people who are also information magnets.

☐ Subscribe to and study appropriate trade magazines.

☐ Attend trade conferences.

☐ Create a resource contact on your local campus.

☐ Share what you learn with others so they, in turn, will share with you.

☐ Do nice things for your "network sources" and enjoy doing it.

☐ Other: _____

_____

_____

The whole idea is to play the information game so that you are not left on the sidelines uninformed.

STRATEGY 2
REFINE AND EXPAND NETWORKING
WITH INFORMATION INTERVIEWS

The more key people you can locate who are willing to discuss your career plans with you, or recommend you to others, the better. With a list of such people "working for you" you start to cover the market and your self-employment program moves into high gear. Not only does networking mean your calling on others, when you create good allies, they may call you. When your Plan B is nearing completion it is time to use networking to put the finishing touches to it. Those in your "camp" can help you refine it now and maintain it in the future. This can best be accomplished through information interviews.

An information interview is designed primarily to "test the market" on various issues such as competency standards, employment conditions, what employers are really seeking, etc. Although an information interview can be the first step finding a new opportunity, it is extremely valuable in its own right. Information interviews usually add fresh names to your networking system. They are also other advantages. Naturally, any information interview that leads to an *employment interview* falls into this category.

The key to gaining an information interview is your own attitude. If you are sincere in seeking information and communicate you will be most appreciative should you receive it, chances are good the interview will be yours. Keep in mind that it is difficult for a person who has achieved status in a career field to turn a newcomer down when they ask for advice you are in a unique position to provide. Here are some tips.

- [ ] Seek people who are in key roles but not directly associated with employment. They receive fewer opportunities to help newcomers.

- [ ] Approach the interview with an open mind so you can discover new possibilities each time.

- [ ] Arrange to meet with them on their conditions (if appropriate offer to host them for lunch).

- [ ] Mention that you have a Plan B and would like advice regarding it.

- [ ] Listen carefully to all suggestions. Ask relevant questions.

- [ ] Ask who else might be in a position to provide you with insights and advice.

- [ ] Always send a "thank you" message.

- [ ] If appropriate, convert the beginning relationship into a mutually rewarding long-term one.

- [ ] Do not "press" beyond the individuals willingness to volunteer information and advice.

STRATEGY 3
EMPLOY AN "ENDLESS CHAIN" NETWORK SYSTEM

Regardless of the kind of networking you have done in the past, consider using an endless chain system. Below is a diagram. Start by listing three key people you feel would be receptive to looking at your Plan B, who are in a position to know of job openings in your specialty. Call each name and make a best effort to arrange a personal meeting. Mention you are completing your Plan B (this may intrigue them) and if you are successful, take it with you.

Once in conversation, request additional names so that you can start your chain. Names provided should be people with whom the first party has an excellent relationship. Always ask if you can use the individual's name. With effort on your part, the "endless chain" networking system can live up to its name. You can keep it operational even after your Plan B turns into Plan A.

"ENDLESS CHAIN" NETWORKING

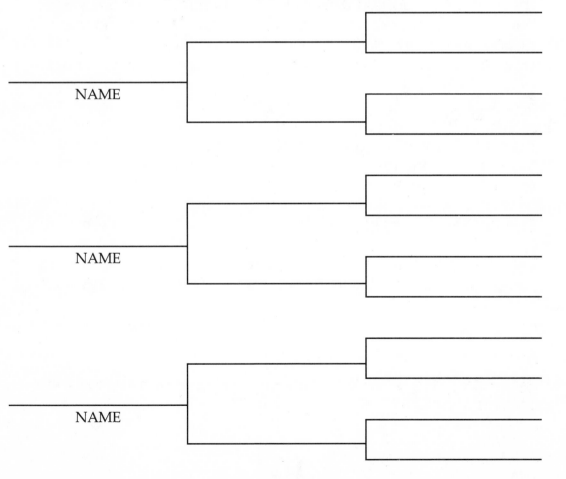

CASE 6: THE CONTACT THAT PAID OFF

Donna had been working undercover on her Plan B for over six months when her boss Mrs. MacCarthy came down hard on her over a mistake a co-worker made. At that moment Donna decided to activate her Plan B.

The first person she decided to call was a Ms. Jamison, a Human Resource director for an electronics firm near her home. Donna met Ms. Jamison through a mutual friend, Hazel, at a conference on job burnout a few weeks earlier. Donna had to make four calls to reach Ms. Jamison (her secretary kept saying she was in a conference) but when the contact was made, Ms. Jamison was most receptive to an information interview and made an appointment for the following week.

The moment Ms. Jamison knew that Donna had almost completed her Plan B she showed immediate interest and they wound up having lunch together. Although Ms. Jamison's firm did not have an opening suitable for Donna, she knew of another firm who did and made arrangements for Donna to be interviewed by a Mr. Sledge.

Donna's qualifications (having been upgraded through her Plan B) were ideal and an employment offer was made which Donna accepted with enthusiasm.

Donna's friend Hazel seemed bored and negative when she heard the story during lunch the following week. Hazel's comments: "You really lucked out, Donna. What happened to you seldom, if ever, happens to others. Frankly, I think networking of all kinds is overrated."

Do you agree with Hazel? Compare your thoughts with those of the author on page 84.

STEP 7
HAVE PLAN—WILL TRAVEL

This final step provides techniques on how to use your Plan B to win a better position either at your present firm or with another organization.

At this stage everything you know or have experienced about job hunting and employment interviews should be brought into play.

IF YOU HAVE DONE YOUR HOMEWORK, YOU WILL HAVE A SIGNIFICANT ADVANTAGE OVER OTHERS.

Like a student graduating from college who has spent hours in placement offices preparing for his or her first serious job-hunting expedition, your Plan B has been prepared and you are ready. You have a Plan B to discuss with a superior inside of your organization or with a prospective employer outside. Study the suggestions below to learn how a Plan B can be used effectively.

| SUGGESTION 1 | **INCLUDE A SUMMARY OF YOUR PLAN B IN YOUR RESUME.** In making a |

INCLUDE A SUMMARY OF YOUR PLAN B IN YOUR RESUME. In making a job change, past history is always important. You communicate this best with a creative resume that incorporates information from your Plan B. A prospective employer may be more interested in your preparation for a new career than your previous experience or education. The best place to include your Plan B is at the very end of your resume so you can highlight what you have done to upgrade yourself recently.

MARKETING YOUR PLAN B

SUGGESTION 2 **INTRODUCE YOUR PLAN B DURING THE INTERVIEW PROCESS.** Using good judgement, introduce your Plan B at the appropriate time. Explain why it was developed. Communicate how you have upgraded your skills. State how you think your Plan B prepared you to contribute more.

SUGGESTION 3 **INVITE QUESTIONS ON YOUR PLAN.** When a prospective employer becomes interested in your career development plan you are doing well in the interview. Rather than being asked questions that may be difficult to answer, the interviewer is asking you questions that will allow you to demonstrate you are a creative person with initiative.

SUGGESTION 4 **USE THE HOME FIELD ADVANTAGE.** This means that through a Plan B you may now have, (perhaps for the first time), an advantage with your present employer. Everything in your plan could help your present employer because you already know the ropes!

SUGGESTION 5 **UNDERSTAND WHY YOUR PLAN B ENHANCES YOUR POTENTIAL.** Anyone who completes a Plan B has demonstrated excellent potential to contribute to productivity because they have demonstrated they are pro active.

SUGGESTION 6 **USE YOUR PLAN B IN A PROFESSIONAL MANNER.** We earlier made the statement that when using a Plan B it is okay to play one end against the middle. In short, you can use your plan to gain the best possible position where you are now. If done openly and honestly, you can use an outside job offer as leverage to do this. Or, you can use a better ''in house'' job offer as leverage to get a better position outside. This should be done without deception so neither party will wind up with a bad taste. Although there is nothing unethical or unprofessional in keeping a Plan B undercover during the preparation period, once you use it as a vehicle to gain a better position, the veil of secrecy should be lifted and it should be used with openness and pride.

CASE 7: PLAN B SEMINARS?

Assume you are Director of Human Resources for a major firm that thus far has been able to withstand most winds of change. As a result, your employees feel rather secure and happy in their roles. Still, you are a Plan B believer. In fact, you have developed one of your own.

Known for your innovative ideas, a few days ago you started thinking about proposing to your management team the idea of having Plan B seminars. The idea appeals to you because you believe only unhappy or unproductive people would choose to leave the organization. Most would view a Plan "B" as a personal development program and thus make a greater contribution. The only thing that worries you is how to convince those on the team you are right.

If this were a real situation, would you take the risk? Make your decision and compare your thinking with that of the author on page 84.

IF YOU DON'T GET STARTED ON YOUR PLAN B NOW (BEFORE YOU FINISH THIS BOOK) IT PROBABLY WON'T HAPPEN.

PART IV

MISCONCEPTIONS ABOUT HAVING A PLAN B

MYTHS ABOUT AN ALTERNATE GROWTH PROGRAM

A PLAN B WILL DISTRACT ME FROM PLAN A: Just the opposite is likely to happen! Looking outside your present career could give it more appeal, not less. Or you might see growth opportunities you have been neglecting. In any event, one plan can help the other. Once involved, you will discover you have time and energy for both.

DOING A PLAN B IS DISCOURAGING: Many individuals think that a Plan B is distasteful. They see it as reading want ads, lining up job prospects, and doing interviews. An alternative growth program is much more than a job-hunting expedition. In fact, developing a Plan B can be exciting for four reasons: (1) You can accomplish the plan while you have the security of a regular job. (2) It is a non-stressful way to lift yourself out of a situation that is leading nowhere. (3) It provides an opportunity to take a fresh look at your future (which is probably brighter than you suspect.) (4) It can cause you to think at a higher level which, in some instances, can turn your life around.

A PLAN B IS TOO RISKY: This myth needs to be exploded quickly. Organizations recognize that employees should protect themselves from the winds of change. Upon learning that a productive employee is working on a Plan B, an enlightened manager should think: ''Perhaps we need to provide Julie with more opportunities here. If we can't, then I wish her luck elsewhere. She is entitled to her future.''

IT IS BETTER TO DO A PLAN B AS A FULL-TIME PROJECT: Some misguided individuals mistakenly believe it is better to start a growth program when they are unemployed. These people fail to recognize the security of having a Plan A (and the income that goes with it) makes it easier to design a superior plan. Outplacement counselors constantly describe the state many unemployed people fall into—a malaise that has a negative impact upon their ability to find a new position. A growth program, developed in advance, enables one to avoid this ''unemployment malaise''.

COMMON MISCONCEPTIONS

PLAN B MEANS MORE FORMAL EDUCATION: A career plan *may* require going back to school, but not always. What about those who already have the skills? Or those who want a similar job with another firm? Or those who want to improve their role through self-learning? Often a Plan B means taking advantage of Plan A learning opportunities now, so a move can be made later.

PLAN B IS FOR YOUNG AGGRESSIVE TYPES: Although a few ambitious young people may see the value of self-programming sooner, this does not mean they need it more. Just the opposite! Restructuring within a business often means the loss of upper or mid-management jobs where salaries are higher and more ''fat'' can be cut. Also, those who have been around longer may have a greater psychological need to get out of a career ''rut''. A Plan B offers the opportunity to ''break from the past'' and start over fresh.

PLAN B MEANS A GEOGRAPHICAL CHANGE: Rather than cause the uprooting of a family, a Plan B can keep you in your present home and location because of advance planning. When people lose their Plan A they often grasp at career straws that can turn their lifestyle upside down. A well-designed growth program can help a person through a major career change with a minimum of disruption. Properly perceived, a Plan B can play a major role in helping you be true to your future.

HUBIE

Hubie graduated from the business program of Ohio State University as a computer programmer. He was encouraged by his professors to join a major company as a trainee and work his way up the management ladder. After years of hard work but uneven progress, Hubie began to challenge the wisdom of his decision. Why should he confine his talents to one firm? Why should he wait to be promoted from within? Why should he hitch his future to a single corporation?

Unexpectedly, Hubie's company merged with a competitor. His job was taken by a person from the other company. Despite all of his educational preparation, productivity, and creative contributions to his company, Hubie was left out in the cold.

Why hadn't he been taught to program his own career so he could protect his future?

WHY SO MANY INDIVIDUALS NEVER DEVELOP A PLAN B

Shocking as it may seem, it is estimated that less than 3 out of every 100 workers have a well-developed alternative career plan. Reasons for this situation of ''non-readiness'' are many. Three of the most obvious, and understandable, are:

1. Higher education places so much emphasis on preparing students to succeed in a Plan A they neglect to point out the need for a backup program. The rationale is that you must have a successful Plan A before you are ready for a Plan B and it is not logical to do both at the same time. ''Win your first career opportunity and after you have settled in, you can worry about a Plan B. First things first.''

2. Many people feel there is something unethical about preparing a Plan B while on a firm's payroll. They feel it shows a lack of loyalty or honesty. On top of this some feel building a Plan B will place their Plan A in jeopardy. ''If your boss discovers you are working on a alternate career possibility, she or he may take a dim view. You may have rendered yourself inelgible for promotions or fair treatment in the future. In case of a reduction, you may be the first to go.'' Many individuals, have yet to discover the mutual advantages of developing alternatives.

3. Perhaps the biggest reason for not developing alternative plans is that most individuals are not motivated to prepare one. It is all they can do to keep a Plan A and their home life going. They can tred water but nothing more. ''Don't talk to me about something better when I am barely hanging to what I have.'' These individuals need to be convinced that having a Plan B will make their Plan A more comfortable while also improving their lifestyle.

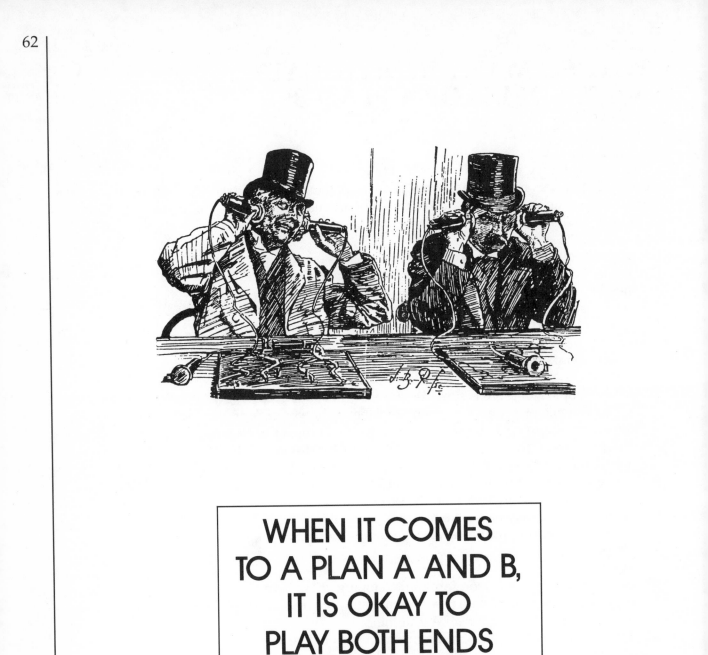

WHEN IT COMES
TO A PLAN A AND B,
IT IS OKAY TO
PLAY BOTH ENDS
AGAINST THE
MIDDLE*

* Providing, of course, you continue to be effective in your Plan A.

HOW WILL OTHERS REACT?

When Jessica called her sister Kim to explain how her strategy got her a higher paying, more creative position Kim replied: ''Great. When we meet next week I want to know all of the details so I can do one of my own.''

When Cody made the decision to activate his Plan B he told the whole story to his boss who replied: ''With all of the changes going on around here you did the right thing. It may come as a surprise but I am in the process of doing one of my own.''

When Dawn received a big promotion she decided to stay with her Plan A but continue to maintain her Plan B. In talking to her boss about her previously secret plan, he replied: ''I am complimented that you would discuss your plan with me and I can see now it had a lot to do with your receiving the promotion. I just hope we can continue to provide you with sufficient challenge to keep you working with us.''

SELF-TEST AHEAD

PRE-TEST

There are many opinions and a few misconceptions about whether a Plan B should be kept secret or communicated to co-workers or superiors. This exercise will help you make your decision. When finished, compare your answers with those below.

True   **False**

_____ _____ 1. Most people are more motivated to reach a secret goal.

_____ _____ 2. There is nothing unethical in preparing a Plan B in secret.

_____ _____ 3. Discussing a Plan B prematurely with co-workers can get it into the grapevine and be counter-productive.

_____ _____ 4. The development of a Plan B can cause one to stay with Plan A.

_____ _____ 5. This book recommends that the reader design, complete, and activate a Plan B while remaining effective with Plan A.

_____ _____ 6. Today most management people are less approving of employees with a Plan B.

_____ _____ 7. A Plan B can cause you to contribute more to an organization.

_____ _____ 8. Most people do not take it seriously when they hear someone is preparing a Plan B.

_____ _____ 9. You and you alone are responsible for your career future.

_____ _____ 10. The time will never arrive when organizations conduct Plan B seminars for their employees.

ANSWERS: 1. F (there is no evidence either way on this). **2.** T (one has the right to prepare a Plan B and it is not unethical as long as she or he remains effective with Plan A) **3.** T (one should be selective in sharing plans on the development of a Plan B). **4.** T (this is one reason why enlightened managers are often in favor of employees preparing a Plan B.) **5.** T (whether one communicates it to superiors is a personal decision). **6.** F (the "winds of change" have caused management to be more approving). **7.** T (the reason this is true will be explained later). **8.** T (this occurs because people talk about back up plans but few actually develop one). **9.** T (and you are free to make a change at any time). **10.** F (a few organizations conduct serious career development programs now).

THE INTRIGUE OF SECRECY

There is nothing unethical about preparing a Plan B while you continue to operate effectively in the job you were hired to perform. For several reasons, however, some individuals prefer to keep their career contingency planning undercover. They do not discuss it with co-workers or superiors. Reasons why secrecy is preferred by some individuals, include:

> "The moment I started working on a Plan B my regular job became easier and more fun. My new attitude was noticed by co-workers. A few thought I had a secret lover. Believe me I enjoyed the mystique my secrecy created."
>
> "I think one is motivated to do a better job with a Plan B when you keep your efforts secret. Knowing you are developing something which you can fall back on frees you to see things differently. You feel proud that you have the guts to do it. It is a little like being the cat that swallowed the canary."
>
> "It was nobody's fault, but when I realized I was boxed in with my Plan A, I started a Plan B. My attitude improved immediately. It was then I decided to keep it secret. I didn't want to jepordize my Plan A and was successful because I recently received a promotion."

Whether you complete your Plan B with or without communication at your Plan A work station is a personal choice. Every individual and situation is different. The approach that motivates you the most is the one recommended.

"Our plans miscarry because they have no aim. When a man does not know what harbor he is making for, no wind is the right wind."

Seneca (4 B.C.-A. D. 65)

PART V

LAUNCHING YOUR PLAN

"Man has a limited biological capacity to change. When this capacity is overwhelmed, the capacity is in future shock."

Alvin Toffler

HAVE A PENCIL IN HAND AS YOU CONSIDER THESE SUGGESTIONS

| SUGGESTION 1 | First read through the MODEL on the next two pages. Although Sara Cottonwood's situation and background may not be similar to yours, you may get some ideas. You are encouraged to follow this format. |

| SUGGESTION 2 | Start your plan now. Understand you will need to do some research later to complete it but just getting started is a big step! |

| SUGGESTION 3 | Consult with those who constitute your support group (or others) as you proceed. View your Plan B as a major project. Six months or more may be required to complete it. |

| SUGGESTION 4 | Be true to your self. The MODEL was designed to provide guidance in the preparation of your own special plan. Yours could be far more sophisticated and demanding. |

A MODEL TO GUIDE YOU

Sara Cottonwood
Graduate Central Arkansas State University
Major: Business Administration
Special competencies: Office management and computer skills
Currently employed as Office Supervisor for Southern Supply Co., Inc.

**STEP 1
COUNT DOWN**

I selected Option 5 because my close friend and co-worker Margaret and I will work together. We plan to have dinner together every Tuesday after work and share the progress we are making.

**STEP 2
HEDGE YOUR
BET**

I checked 8 of the streamlining suggestions and will follow through on them in the next few weeks. In addition, I intend to do the following.
Delegate more to others in my office.
Make a list of daily priorities so that
I have a minimum of 30 minutes each
noon hour to work on my Plan B.
Ask my superior to assign my credit union
responsibilities to another manager.
Demonstrate more leadership so others will
not flood me with work they should be
doing themselves.

**STEP 3
YOU'VE GOT
TO BE
KIDDING!**

I have isolated the following learning opportunities where I work and pursue them when time permits and the situation is right.

Negotiation Strategies Workshop March 6th & 7th
Leadership Seminar April 16th
Word Processing Software, Learn via company tutorial

SARA COTTONWOOD'S PLAN B

STEP 4
QUALIFY FIRST!

Here are the competency standards that I intend to reach during the next six months.

Upgrade computer application skills in the area of word processing and data base management

Improve my communication and counseling skills

STEP 5
DECISION TIME

Each semester until my Plan B is complete I will enroll at the university for courses in database management. Successful completion of these courses will make me proficient in the latest generation of relational databases.

I recognize that I need to improve my management skills so I will do this both by attending company seminars and at night on a self-paced basis. I will subscribe to: OFFICE MANAGEMENT

STEP 6
CREATIVE
NETWORKING

I plan to build my network on an ongoing basis. I intend to add one person per week to a list composed of key individuals. Each will be in a position to give me both guidance and contacts. I anticipate at least 50% of these key people will come from my trade group (NOMA). To improve my accessibility to such people I intend to become an officer in that association. I now have three people on my list. I hope to wind up with 15.

STEP 7
HAVE PLAN—
WILL TRAVEL

Although I may change my mind when the time arrives, I plan to activate my Plan B when it is finished. I like the challenge of doing this while I continue to make progress with my present firm. My goal is to increase my annual income by $10,000.00 or more (with comparable benefits). When the time is right I will speed up my networking and use my Plan B for both information and actual job interviews. Frankly, I am more excited about the future than at any time since I graduated from college seven years ago. Margaret feels the same way.

Wish me luck!

PLAN B WORKSHEETS

START NOW AND FINISH LATER

Your name: _____

Anticipated date of completion: _____

STEP 1 **COUNT DOWN**	I am going with Option #_____. My reasons are: _____ _____

STEP 2 **HEDGE YOUR** **BET**	To free myself to develop my Plan B I intend to streamline my present job in the following ways: _____ _____ _____ _____

STEP 3 **YOU'VE GOT** **TO BE** **KIDDING!**	I have isolated the following learning opportunities where I work. _____ _____ _____ _____

WORKSHEETS (Continued)

| STEP 4
QUALIFY FIRST! | Here are the competency standards that I intend to reach. |

_____

_____

_____

| STEP 5
DECISION TIME | I will enroll in and complete the following courses: |

_____

_____

_____

My self-help learning program at home will include:

_____

_____

_____

| STEP 6
CREATIVE
NETWORKING | My networking strategy will be. I will or will not use the endless chain networking system. |

_____

_____

_____

| STEP 7
HAVE PLAN—
WILL TRAVEL | Whether or not I activate my Plan B when completed will depend upon: |

_____

_____

_____

WHEN DOUBTS REMAIN

It is natural for some readers to remain skeptical about the Plan B
concept. Is it really worth all of the time and effort? Would there
really be a substantial payoff for me?

Obviously, you must find agreement within yourself on the value of
a Plan B. To help you do this, three hypothetical cases are
presented. Please read, react, and then compare your views with
those of the author.

CASE 8: JEREMY & PAUL

Jeremy and Paul's relationship was work oriented. They have been in the same department, doing the same basic work for four years. Although both are the same age, have similar backgrounds, and are married with children, they did not see each other socially.

Last year rumors persisted that their firm would go through a major restructuring and some departments would be eliminated. Jeremy took the rumors seriously and encouraged Paul to do the same. In fact, he suggested they help each other develop a Plan B. Paul showed no interest, so Jeremy independently started work on one. Among other things, it included going back to school to upgrade his skills and the beginnings of a job search.

When the announcement was made that their department had been eliminated, Paul was in a state of shock. He asked Jeremy to have a beer with him that afternoon. "Jer", said Paul, "I'm really scared about the future. In addition to our mortgage, we owe on our cars and have other bills. I guess we should have taken those rumors seriously." Jeremy replied: "I did, Paul but you will recall you were not interested at the time. Let me tell you what I have been doing and perhaps it may help you get started."

Is it too late for Paul to do a Plan B? Please write out your answer in the spaces provided and turn to page 84 to compare your views.

_____

_____

_____

_____

CASE 9: GERALDINE

Gerry, newly employed by Trac Corporation, was discouraged by the complacency of her more experienced co-workers. Sensing that her future was limited at Trac, she started work on a Plan B. A major part of her strategy was to take advantage of her present job by learning more. She asked to learn how to operate the latest equipment. She asked for more responsibility when new programs were introduced. This helped provide more knowledge and contributed to her positive attitude. Gerry kept her personal productivity high, not to impress her superiors, but to prepare herself for another career opportunity.

One morning, to her surprise, Geraldine was invited into the division manager's office and offered the position of department manager. The new position would give her a 20% increase in salary and new opportunities to learn.

Is this case realistic? Is it possible that in preparing for a better job elsewhere an employee can receive an unusual opportunity at home? Please express your views and compare with those of the author on page 84.

_____

_____

_____

_____

CASE 10: LARRY

Almost everyone around the plant knew about the conflict between Larry and his boss. Unfortunately, it was so hard on Larry that he required professional help. Things started to get better only after the counselor suggested that Larry start making plans to free himself from a situation that was untenable for both he and his family.

It came as no surprise when Larry resigned. What did surprise everyone was hearing that Larry had developed a Plan B and had an offer to join a competitive organization with a superior position. In discussing the situation later with a former colleague, Larry said: "It was obvious months ago that I could not build a good relationship so I took the only door open to me. I kept learning and protecting myself while I did some upgrading and serious networking. Do I have hard feelings? Just the opposite. Without the problem I would not have been motivated to do a Plan B in the first place."

What was the real advantage of a Plan B to Larry? Please write out your answer and compare with that found on page 84.

_____

_____

_____

_____

_____

PART VI

MAINTENANCE IDEAS!

We earlier compared a Plan B to an insurance policy or having money wisely invested. When it comes to maintaining a completed Plan B it might be best to compare it to a fine automobile. Just like any mechanical device, a plan can deteriorate and become inoperative if not used properly or neglected.

To maintain an automobile you must put in gas and oil, get an occasional lube job and keep the engine tuned. Now and then some repairs will be necessary. To maintain a Plan B you must keep your skills at high standards, continue your networking efforts, schedule information interviews on a regular basis, and review and revise your Plan B as required. Your Plan B shouldn't gather cobwebs.

Listed below are some Plan B maintenance tips. Please place a ✔ opposite those you intend to honor.

☐ Keep your plan and this book in a prominent place as a reminder that you have the equivalent of a career insurance policy providing you keep your Plan B up to date.

☐ Thumb through your plan every three months to see if deletions or additions need to be made.

☐ Remind yourself that your plan is, in effect, your mental health protection plan. It provides you with both freedom and security.

☐ Your plan should pay your interest. That is, it should provide you with psychological dividends like increased motivation, confidence, and a greater willingness to take risks.

☐ One of the best ways to maintain a Plan B is to help someone else do one. In doing this, you may discover a weakness in your own.

☐ An ideal time to do a "maintenance check" is when you return from a professional meeting or trade conference. New trends, compentency standards, and additions to your network should be added.

78

COMMON MISTAKES

Four common mistakes are listed below. Now that you have almost finished this book, which one are you most apt to make? Place a ✔ in the appropriate box.

☐ **UNDERESTIMATING THE EXCITEMENT AND INTRIGUE INVOLVED.** Many people consider developing and maintaining a Plan B as work. They are wrong. Like taking a first trip in a balloon, a well developed plan can provide a new perspective on your career and future. This happens because you free yourself from organizational dependency. It's a greet feeling!

☐ **FIGURING YOU HAVE A PLAN WHEN YOU DON'T.** Now that you know what is involved (seven steps) you may not make this mistake. Still, you may be tempted to take too many shortcuts. You do not want to pay premiums on an insurance policy that you can't collect on when the chips are down.

☐ **WAITING TOO LONG TO GET STARTED.** If you were to receive notice today that your job will be eliminated in 30 days you waited too long. Few good plans can be prepared and completed in less than three months.

☐ **REFUSING TO SEE THE FULL VALUE.** Some people persist in thinking that a Plan B does little more than win you a promotion or another job. In addition, a true plan can enhance your Plan A, contribute to fulfilling your life goals, and provide you with a new, exciting philosophy of work.

SELF-QUIZ

Please answer the following true-false questions.

TRUE	FALSE

_____   _____   1. You can't have a Plan B without a Plan A.

_____   _____   2. The value of a Plan B does not depend upon whether or not it is exercised.

_____   _____   3. Having a secret Plan B is unethical.

_____   _____   4. A Plan B will provide you with the career you should have chosen years ago.

_____   _____   5. The farther you fall behind in job skills of your specialty the longer it will take you to complete a Plan B.

_____   _____   6. Networking is building strong mutually rewarding relationships with people who are in a position to help you activate your Plan B when it is ready.

_____   _____   7. An information interview is designed to keep you in touch with the job market and those competencies required.

_____   _____   8. Networking and information interviews are a minor part of developing a Plan B.

_____   _____   9. A Plan B frequently sends the preparer back to college.

_____   _____   10. Some individuals improve their skills through assuming more responsibility in their current job.

SELF-QUIZ (Continued)

TRUE	FALSE

———— ———— 11. Self-learning at home can sometimes contribute as much to a successful Plan B as formal learning on campus.

———— ———— 12. A good time to construct a Plan B is while you are drawing unemployment insurance.

———— ———— 13. The moment your Plan B is operational it becomes your Plan A and you need another Plan B.

———— ———— 14. The best way to make yourself more ''marketable'' is to improve your job skills.

———— ———— 15. The three best ways to improve your special competencies are to: (1) learn more at your present job (2) take college courses (3) engage in self-learning at home.

———— ———— 16. Once a Plan B is complete it does not require maintenance for at least a year.

———— ———— 17. A Plan B is essentially a philosophy toward work.

———— ———— 18. Many colleges now offer seminars on the significance of having a Plan B and how to develop one.

———— ———— 19. Lack of motivation is the number one reason most people do not have a Plan B.

———— ———— 20. Restructuring, mergers, and relocations are a passing fad and will slow down in the future.

SELF-QUIZ (Continued)

TRUE	FALSE	
_____	_____	21. It is estimated that less than 3% of those employed full-time have a workable Plan B.
_____	_____	22. The program presented in this book contains a seven-step process that can be completed in a few weeks.
_____	_____	23. Doing a Plan B is all work and no play.
_____	_____	24. The endless chain system is an interviewing technique.
_____	_____	25. A Plan B is designed to improve your Plan A while it prepares you to lose it.

EACH CORRECT ANSWER IS WORTH FOUR POINTS.

TOTAL SCORE [ ]

(Correct answers on the following page.)

ANSWERS TO SELF-QUIZ

COMPARE YOUR ANSWERS WITH THOSE OF THE AUTHOR:

1. TRUE — A plan A is your present career role, a Plan B is an alternative yet to be exercised.
2. TRUE — Sometimes developing a Plan B motivates one to do a better job with Plan A and a promotion makes it undesirable to move.
3. FALSE — There is nothing unethical about protecting your future from the modern winds of change.
4. FALSE — Finding the right career is a separate matter. A Plan B, however, can lead you in the right direction.
5. TRUE — When you fall too far behind going back to college may be necessary and this takes time.
6. TRUE — Advance networking is a critical part of any Plan B.
7. TRUE — This is necessary so you will know when your Plan B is complete and operational.
8. FALSE — A major part!
9. TRUE — Taking a college course (or earning a degree) is often the only way to reach one's Plan B goals.
10. TRUE — These are very perceptive and smart individuals.
11. TRUE — Self-learning at home is on the increase. More publications are available.
12. FALSE — You can't do a Plan B without a Plan A.
13. TRUE — This means you may develop more than one Plan B.
14. TRUE — In most fields, skill improvement (retraining) is increasingly necessary.
15. TRUE — Steps 5, 6, & 7 in the Plan B process.
16. FALSE — Like maintaining an automobile, frequent repairs and tuning are required.
17. TRUE — A Plan B has both a pragmatic and philosophical side.
18. FALSE — Hopefully they may do so in the future.
19. TRUE — Most people talk Plan B but actually do little in constructing one.
20. FALSE — Most experts believe the trend will continue for at least ten years—perhaps to the next century.
21. TRUE — The author believes this low percentage figure will increase substantially in the next few years.
22. FALSE — Seven steps, yes; but there is too much involved to complete a good plan in a few weeks.
23. FALSE — Doing a plan can and should also be fun.
24. FALSE — The "endless chain" system is a networking technique.
25. TRUE — This is a paradox some find difficult to accept.

AUTHOR'S SUGGESTED ANSWERS TO CASES

CASE 1: RICHARD

If both Richard and his wife Marie are giving consideration to the Uncle George possibility, it seems that Marie questions her ability to provide enough motivation. If Uncle George is the best ''model'' Richard has available, and if Uncle George is willing to go with an informal contract, the author feels this might be the best motivator. This arrangement would be less complex to start with and easier for Richard to maintain. Although Richard can communicate his plan to the other people (and they can be of help along the way) his commitment to Uncle George could provide 90% of the motivation required.

CASE 2: CONFLICT

James does not see the long-range, true value of a Plan B. He refuses to see that he can make changes now that will help him no matter what happens in the future. James subscribes to the old-fashioned theory that the only way to get a better job is to dump your present one first. Gregg believes you can use a present job, no matter how unpleasant it may be, to gain a better one.

CASE 3: ATTITUDE REVERSAL

It is doubtful that Tanya will be able to turn things around in her present job. Because of this, it might be best for her not to expect so much from herself but rather do other things to prepare a Plan B. Although it is best to make all possible improvements with Plan A while working on Plan B, all of the major behavioral reverses she must make are not realistic.

CASE 4: JACK'S PROBLEM

It depends just how much improvement Jack must make to bring his skills up to standard. If the gap is extremely wide, it might be best for him to return to campus full time. Once caught up, Jack can try for a fresh start. If, however, the gap is modest, Jack's three step approach can work and will produce less strain on himself.

AUTHOR'S SUGGESTED ANSWERS TO CASES
(Continued)

CASE 5: CHALLENGE FOR MARY

Mary is lucky that she has such a good opportunity to carve out a practical career for herself. She should find out, however how long it would be before she could be transferred into the marketing department. The combination of college work, self-study, and on-the-job learning is ideal. With Mary's background, progress should be speedy.

CASE 6: THE CONTACT THAT PAID OFF

Hazel is expressing sour grapes because she has never given networking a chance. True, networking can lead one up blind alleys, it only takes one right contact to wind up a winner. Donna is to be congratulated for being so persistant.

CASE 7: PLAN B SEMINARS

The author is of the opinion that any large organization, especially one that is downsizing, would benefit from offering employees such a seminar. There would be some exceptions, but generally speaking helping people develop a Plan B would increase productivity and encourage them to remain rather than leave.

CASE 8: JEREMY & PAUL

It is not to late for Paul to get started on finding a new job but it is too late for him to prepare a Plan B. The reader is reminded that a Plan B is developed ahead of time while the individual still has a Plan A. Jeremy stands a chance of finding a better job. Paul may have to initially settle for something beneath his previous responsibilities.

CASE 9: GERALDINE

The author contends that this case is highly realistic because Geraldine's Plan B caused her to live up to her potential while the other employees drifted along. Thus Geraldine's performance stood out. It was not important for management to know Geraldine has a Plan B.

CASE 10: LARRY

When Larry started to develop a departure plan he kept himself from being victimized. Without a plan, Larry could have become so bitter and frustrated that he would have been damaged. A Plan B can help one do a better job of surviving until a new opportunity opens up. Sometimes a Plan B is the only way to turn a bad situation into an excellent one.

APPENDIX I

USING THE PLAN B APPROACH TO WIN THE RIGHT PART-TIME RETIREMENT JOB.

A growing number of individuals over 50 have lost jobs due to the winds of change. Others are unhappy because of human conflicts and/or the downgrading of their responsibilities. Still others realize they need job involvement after retirement for either financial or psychological reasons. The result of all this is that many employees within distance of retirement need a special kind of Plan B.

Although highly qualified in the field of printing and graphics Lee, at 53, is finding it difficult to locate a challenging replacement. His previous position was eliminated. Result? He is developing a Plan B that will move him into retirement sooner than he and his wife had anticipated.

Ruth, a widow of 60, needs to supplement her retirement income. Result? She is learning new skills and upgrading old ones to find a part-time job that will take her to 65 and Medicare coverage.

Ken is 55 and under great pressure from a superior who would like nothing better than to see him retire. Result? Tired of waiting for a ''golden handshake'', Ken is busy working on a Plan B that will provide additional retirement income through a part-time job.

Notice that neither Lee, Ruth, or Ken *desire* a full time job after retirement. All have a financial package sufficient to make do providing they can create a supplemental income that falls within their comfort zones. For many people, this is a most difficult challenge. They want to work, but not full time. They want a job, but one with less pressure. They want a position with some dignity and which will provide enough income or creative involvement to make it worthwhile. Research shows that many financially secure retirees still need some form of work to keep them challenged.

LAST CHANCE TO BE TRUE TO YOUR FUTURE

Retirement is the last chance an individual has to be true to his or her future. Finding the *right* part-time position is critical. In some cases this may mean doing a late-in-life career search to find a fresh, creative career. For example, many retirees go into business for themselves. Those who elect to work for others need all the job-finding skills of a recent college graduate. Perhaps more.

NOTHING MAKES MORE SENSE THAT USING THE SEVEN STEP PLAN B PROCESS. For example, assume you would like to retire next year from your current job (Plan A) but will need a challenging part-time job (for either money or psychological reasons). If you return to page 23 and go through the seven steps a second time, you will see (with some variations) just how applicable the process can be to your special situation. To assist you in doing this, the seven steps are adjusted and augmented below. It is suggested you read the step in the body of the text first and then read the suggestions below.

STEP 1: COUNT DOWN. Face it, you need as much support in preparing a retirement program as you do for a Plan B. Maybe more! Your best approach would be to sign up for a pre-retirement seminar (if your company does not offer one you might enroll in one at a local college). This could become a support group for you. Your Plan B effort would give your comprehensive retirement plan special help in an area where it is most needed. If married, it is strongly recommended that you work as a team with your spouse. Other support people may also be needed.

EACH STEP WORKS!

STEP 2: HEDGE YOUR BET. There are two reasons why, as a possible retiree you should consider streamlining your job. First, simplify things at work to get rid of some pressure. This is traditional and often expected by employers. Second, you need extra time (both on the job and at home) to do retirement planning. The more efficient you become at work, the more excited you will be about retirement! Go to it!

STEP 3: YOU'VE GOT TO BE KIDDING. Just because you are thinking about retirement is not a signal for you to stop learning. Just the opposite! Now is the time to learn skills from your present job that will help you qualify for a post-retirement job. Can you transfer present skills or do you need to learn new ones? What can you learn now that will help you later? It is natural for people about to retire to stop learning. This is never wise. Give this step some thought!

STEP 4: QUALIFY FIRST. Many people who retire are forced to take part-time jobs beneath their capabilities. This, of course, is free choice (some like getting away from the pressures). Most retirees however want a mental challenge and the financial rewards that go along with accomplishments. If this sounds like you, then the time to qualify for a new career or position is while you are still on a payroll. The way to do this, of course, is to find the job you really want ahead of time. Then start the qualification process. This is especially true if you intend to start your own business.

IT'S NEVER TOO LATE!

STEP 5: DECISION TIME. More and more individuals approaching retirement are returning to college to learn new skills or bring old ones up to date. Some plan to turn hobbies into part-time endeavors. Others will learn skills so they can build boats, homes, or do repair work at their own pace. Still others will develop office skills so they can find part-time jobs near their homes. If a local university or community college does not offer what is needed, self-instruction is often the answer. Some will do limited moonlighting, (like working as a small appliance repair person two or three nights per week).

STEP 6: CREATIVE NETWORKING. Everything in this step applies to a potential retiree! Although an employment agency might come up with the kind of part-time job you seek, it is unlikely because most agencies work primarily with those seeking full-time jobs. Thus it is more important for you to take the initative. Through networking and information interviews you need to determine the job situation you desire. This means maintaining your confidence and not selling yourself short because of age. Also, do not permit prospective employers to take advantage of you with lower wages than deserved or expectation of more work than is reasonable. Networking is the answer and the sooner you start the better!

STEP 7: HAVE PLAN-WILL TRAVEL. As a soon to be retiree, you may not want to travel (where you decide to retire is usually more important than any part-time job). Your Plan B will be the key. In keeping an information or employment interview, simply tell your contact what you plan to do. Ask if anything fits both your needs and theirs.

Of course, ''The Proof Is In The Pudding.'' The seven steps provide strategy, but only you can develop a written plan and implement it.

As you do this, you may wish to use the best selling book COMFORT ZONES; A PRACTICAL GUIDE TO RETIREMENT PLANNING as a resource to your retirement planning. COMFORT ZONES is a complete guide to retirement (it covers both financial and emotional aspects) and can be ordered from CRISP PUBLICATIONS, 95 First Street, Los Altos, California 94022 for just $15.00 which includes postage.

ABOUT BE TRUE TO YOUR FUTURE

The author of this book (PLAN B:) has written two companion volumes titled I GOT THE JOB! and CAREER DISCOVERY. Both of these titles are in the "Fifty-Minute" format and may be ordered using the form on page 91.

These three books represent a continuum that allows a reader to establish a life goal and select a career based on it (CAREER DISCOVERY), find the best available job within that career (I GOT THE JOB!) and stay competitive in that job (PLAN B: PROTECTING YOUR CAREER FROM THE WINDS OF CHANGE).

Learn for yourself why this series can help you develop better life planning skills.

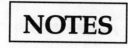

NOTES

FOR OTHER FIFTY-MINUTE SELF-STUDY BOOKS
SEE ORDER FORM AT THE BACK OF THE BOOK.

NOTES

FOR OTHER FIFTY-MINUTE SELF-STUDY BOOKS
SEE ORDER FORM AT THE BACK OF THE BOOK.

NOTES

NOTES

ABOUT THE FIFTY-MINUTE SERIES

"Every so often an idea emerges that is so simple and appealing, people wonder why it didn't come along sooner. The Fifty-Minute series is just such an idea. Excellent!"

> Mahaliah Levine, Vice President for
> Training and Development
> Dean Witter Reynolds, Inc.

WHAT IS A FIFTY-MINUTE BOOK?
—Fifty-Minute books are brief, soft-covered, "self-study" titles covering a wide variety of topics pertaining to business and self-improvement. They are reasonably priced, ideal for formal training, excellent for self-study and perfect for remote location training.

"A Fifty-Minute book gives the reader fundamentals that can be applied on the job, even before attending a formal class"

> Lynn Baker, Manager of Training
> Fleming Corporation

WHY ARE FIFTY-MINUTE BOOKS UNIQUE?
—Because of their format. Designed to be "read with a pencil," the basics of a subject can be quickly grasped and applied through a series of hands-on activities, exercises and cases.

"Fifty-Minute books are the best new publishing idea in years. They are clear, practical, concise and affordable—perfect for today's world."

> Leo Hauser, Past President
> ASTD

HOW MANY FIFTY-MINUTE BOOKS ARE THERE?
—Those listed on the following pages at this time. Additional titles are always in development. For more information write to **Crisp Publications, Inc., 95 First Street, Los Altos, CA 94022.**

THE FIFTY-MINUTE SERIES

Quantity	Title	Code #	Price	Amount
	MANAGEMENT TRAINING			
	Successful Negotiation	09-2	$7.95	
	Personal Performance Contracts	12-2	$7.95	
	Team Building	16-5	$7.95	
	Effective Meeting Skills	33-5	$7.95	
	An Honest Day's Work	39-4	$7.95	
	Managing Disagreement Constructively	41-6	$7.95	
	Training Managers To Train	43-2	$7.95	
	The Fifty-Minute Supervisor	58-0	$7.95	
	Leadership Skills For Women	62-9	$7.95	
	Problem Solving & Decision Making	63-7	$7.95	
	Coaching & Counseling For Supervisors	68-8	$7.95	
	Management Dilemmas: A Guide to Business Ethics	69-6	$7.95	
	Understanding Organizational Change	71-8	$7.95	
	Project Management	75-0	$7.95	
	Managing Organizational Change	80-7	$7.95	
	Managing A Diverse Workforce	85-8	$7.95	
	PERSONNEL TRAINING & HUMAN RESOURCE MANAGEMENT			
	Effective Performance Appraisals	11-4	$7.95	
	Quality Interviewing	13-0	$7.95	
	Personal Counseling	14-9	$7.95	
	Job Performance and Chemical Dependency	27-0	$7.95	
	New Employee Orientation	46-7	$7.95	
	Professional Excellence for Secretaries	52-1	$7.95	
	Guide To Affirmative Action	54-8	$7.95	
	Writing A Human Resource Manual	70-X	$7.95	
	COMMUNICATIONS			
	Effective Presentation Skills	24-6	$7.95	
	Better Business Writing	25-4	$7.95	
	The Business of Listening	34-3	$7.95	
	Writing Fitness	35-1	$7.95	
	The Art of Communicating	45-9	$7.95	
	Technical Presentation Skills	55-6	$7.95	
	Making Humor Work For You	61-0	$7.95	
	Better Technical Writing	64-5	$7.95	
	Using Visual Aids in Business	77-7	$7.95	
	Influencing Others: A Practical Guide	84-X	$7.95	
	SELF-MANAGEMENT			
	Balancing Home And Career	10-6	$7.95	
	Mental Fitness: A Guide to Emotional Health	15-7	$7.95	
	Personal Financial Fitness	20-3	$7.95	
	Attitude: Your Most Priceless Possession	21-1	$7.95	
	Personal Time Management	22-X	$7.95	

(Continued on next page)

THE FIFTY-MINUTE SERIES

Quantity	Title	Code #	Price	Amount
	SELF-MANAGEMENT (CONTINUED)			
	Preventing Job Burnout	23-8	$7.95	
	Successful Self-Management	26-2	$7.95	
	Developing Positive Assertiveness	38-6	$7.95	
	Time Management And The Telephone	53-X	$7.95	
	Memory Skills In Business	56-4	$7.95	
	Developing Self-Esteem	66-1	$7.95	
	Creativity In Business	67-X	$7.95	
	Quality Awareness: A Personal Guide To Professional Standards	72-6	$7.95	
	Managing Personal Change	74-2	$7.95	
	Speedreading For Better Productivity	78-5	$7.95	
	Winning At Human Relations	86-6	$7.95	
	Stop Procrastinating	88-2	$7.95	
	SALES TRAINING/QUALITY CUSTOMER SERVICE			
	Sales Training Basics	02-5	$7.95	
	Restaurant Server's Guide	08-4	$7.95	
	Quality Customer Service	17-3	$7.95	
	Telephone Courtesy And Customer Service	18-1	$7.95	
	Professional Selling	42-4	$7.95	
	Customer Satisfaction	57-2	$7.95	
	Telemarketing Basics	60-2	$7.95	
	Calming Upset Customers	65-3	$7.95	
	Managing A Quality Service Organization	83-1	$7.95	
	ENTREPRENEURSHIP			
	Marketing Your Consulting Or Professional Services	40-8	$7.95	
	Starting Your Small Business	44-0	$7.95	
	Publicity Power	82-3	$7.95	
	CAREER GUIDANCE & STUDY SKILLS			
	Study Skills Strategies	05-X	$7.95	
	Career Discovery	07-6	$7.95	
	Plan B: Protecting Your Career From The Winds of Change	48-3	$7.95	
	I Got The Job!	59-9	$7.95	
	OTHER CRISP INC. BOOKS			
	Comfort Zones: A Practical Guide For Retirement Planning	00-9	$13.95	
	Stepping Up To Supervisor	11-8	$13.95	
	The Unfinished Business Of Living: Helping Aging Parents	19-X	$12.95	
	Managing Performance	23-7	$18.95	
	Be True To Your Future: A Guide to Life Planning	47-5	$13.95	
	Up Your Productivity	49-1	$10.95	
	How To Succeed In A Man's World	79-3	$7.95	
	Practical Time Management	275-4	$13.95	
	Copyediting: A Practical Guide	51-3	$18.95	

☐ Send volume discount information.

☐ Please send me a catalog.

	Amount
Total (from other side)	
Shipping ($1.50 first book, $.50 per title thereafter)	
California Residents add 7% tax	
Total	

Ship to: _____

_____

_____

_____

Phone number: _____

Bill to: _____

_____

_____

_____

P.O. # _____

**All orders except those with a P.O.# must be prepaid.
For more information Call (415) 949-4888 or FAX (415) 949-1610.**

||||

2611